WASSERSTEIN

in an hour

by Alexis Greene

PLAYWRIGHTS in an hour
enhancing the experience of theater
SMITH A KRAUS - HANOVER, NEW HAMPSHIRE - SMITHANDKRAUS.COM

With grateful thanks to Carl R. Mueller, whose fascinating introductions to his translations of the Greek and German playwrights provided inspiration for this series.

Published by In an Hour Books
An imprint of Smith and Kraus, Inc.
177 Lyme Road, Hanover, NH 03755
inanhourbooks.com smithandkraus.com

Know the playwright, love the play

ISBN-10 1936232871
ISBN-13 9781936232871
Library of Congress Control Number 2012955917

For performance rights, contact Dramatists Play Service,
440 Park Ave. S., New York, NY 10016
(www.dramatists.com)
(212-683-8960).

CONTENTS

WHY PLAYWRIGHTS IN AN HOUR?

This new series by Smith and Kraus Publishers titled Playwrights in an Hour has a dual purpose for being: one academic, the other general. For the general reader, this volume, as well as the many others in the series, offers in compact form the information needed for a basic understanding and appreciation of the works of each volume's featured playwright. Which is not to say that there don't exist volumes on end devoted to each playwright under consideration. But inasmuch as few are blessed with enough time to read the splendid scholarship that is available, a brief, highly focused accounting of the playwright's life and work is in order. The central feature of the series, a thirty- to forty-page essay, integrates the playwright into the context of his or her time and place. The volumes, though written to high standards of academic integrity, are accessible in style and approach to the general reader as well as to the student and, of course, to the theater professional and theatergoer. These books will serve for the brushing up of one's knowledge of a playwright's career, to the benefit of theater work or theatergoing. The Playwrights in an Hour series represents all periods of Western theater: Aeschylus to Shakespeare to Wedekind to Ibsen to Williams to Beckett, and on to the great contemporary playwrights who continue to offer joy and enlightenment to a grateful world.

Carl R. Mueller
School of Theater, Film and Television
Department of Theater
University of California, Los Angeles

WASSERSTEIN IN A MINUTE

Age	Date	
–	1950	Enter Wendy Wasserstein.
1	1951	*I Love Lucy* makes its debut on CBS-TV.
7	1957	*I Love Lucy* ends on CBS-TV.
11	1961	President Kennedy asks Congress for $531 million to put a man on the moon.
12	1962	The U.S. and the Soviet Union face off during the Cuban Missile Crisis.
13	1963	Betty Friedan's *The Feminine Mystique* is published; President Kennedy is assassinated.
14	1964	*Funny Girl* opens on Broadway.
15	1965	The Newark Museum opens the exhibit Women Artists in America: 1707-1964.
19	1969	Wasserstein takes a drama course at Smith College.
23	1973	Wasserstein enters the Yale School of Drama.
28	1978	The first in vitro-fertilized baby is born in England.
29	1979	Margaret Thatcher becomes the 1st female prime minister of the UK.
30	1980	The Me!Me!Me! decade begins; Ronald Reagan is elected President.
32	1982	Wasserstein's article "The Itch to Hitch" appears in Mademoiselle.
33	1983	3,000 AIDS cases are reported in the U.S.
34	1984	The state of Mississippi belatedly ratifies the 19th Amendment, giving women the right to vote.

A snapshot of the playwright's world. From historical to pop-culture and the literary landscape of the time, this brief list catalogues events that directly or indirectly impacted the playwright's writing.

35	1985	William Hoffman's *As Is*, one of the first plays about AIDS, opens on Broadway.
37	1987	9,756 deaths from AIDS reported in NYC; the anti-AIDS drug AZT is allowed to be prescribed in the U.S.
39	1989	*The Heidi Chronicles* transfers to Broadway, wins the Tony Award® for Best Play; Wasserstein wins the Pulitzer Prize for Drama.
40	1990	Iraq invades Kuwait.
42	1992	William Jefferson Clinton becomes President of the United States; Lincoln Center produces *The Sisters Rosensweig*.
44	1994	Tony Kushner's *Angels in America: Perestroika* wins the Tony Award® for Best Play.
45	1995	President Clinton begins a sexual relationship with intern Monica Lewinsky.
48	1998	The U.S. House of Representatives votes to impeach President Clinton.
49	1999	Wasserstein gives birth to Lucy Jane. Wasserstein; the U.S. Senate acquits Clinton.
50	2000	Lincoln Center Theater produces Wasserstein's *Old Money*; George W. Bush becomes President of the United States.
51	2001	The World Trade Center is destroyed by terrorists.
52	2002	Congress authorizes military force against Iraq; Wasserstein begins treatments for cancer.
54	2004	George W. Bush is elected to a second Presidential term; Abu Ghraib photographs are leaked.
55	2006	Exit Wendy Wasserstein.

WASSERSTEIN: HER WORKS

Full-Length Plays

> *Uncommon Women and Others*
> *Isn't It Romantic*
> *The Heidi Chronicles*
> *The Sisters Rosensweig*
> *An American Daughter*
> *Old Money*
> *Third*

One-Act Plays

> *Any Woman Can't*
> *Happy Birthday*
> *Montpelier Pa-Zazz*
> Seven One-act Plays (Includes *Bette and Me, Boy Meets Girl, The Man in a Case, Medea* [co-authored with Christopher Durang], *Tender Offer, Waiting for Philip Glass,* and *Workout.*)
> *Welcome to My Rash*
> *Third*

Cabaret and Musical Theater

> *When Dinah Shore Ruled the Earth* (with Christopher Durang)
> *Miami*
> *Bette and Me*
> *Medea* (with Christopher Durang)
> *An American in Paris* (adaptation for Broadway)
> *Pamela's First Musical* (music Cy Coleman, lyrics David Zippel)

This section presents a complete list of the playwright's works in chronological order. Titles appearing in another language indicate that they were first written and premiered in that language]

Librettos for Ballet and Opera
> *The Nutcracker*
> *The Festival of Regrets* (composer Deborah Drattell)
> *Best Friends* (composer Deborah Drattell)

Television Scripts
> *Uncommon Women and Others*
> *The Heidi Chronicles*
> *An American Daughter*
> *The Sisters Rosensweig*

Film Scripts
> *The Sorrows of Gin* (adapted from the short story by John Cheever)
> *House of Husbands*
> *Isn't It Romantic*
> *Dancing Girls*
> *Public Relations*
> *The Object of My Affection*
> *The Sisters Rosensweig*

Children's Book
> *Pamela's First Musical* (Illustrations by Andrew Jackness)

Non-Fiction
> *Shiksa Goddess, or, How I Spent My Forties*
> *Bachelor Girls*
> *Sloth*

Novel
> *Elements of Style* (published posthumously)

ONSTAGE WITH WASSERSTEIN

Theater

Joan Allen, American actor
André Bishop, American artistic director
Alma Cuervo, American actor
Christopher Durang, American playwright
Gerald Gutierrez, American director
Heidi Landesman, American scenic designer
Terence McNally, American playwright
Daniel Sullivan, American director

Arts

Lucille Ball, American comedian
Belle Barth, American comedian
Kitty Carlisle Hart, American arts administrator
and philanthropist
Annie Leibovitz, American photographer
Bette Midler, American actress and singer
Jerome Robbins, American choreographer
Julian Schnabel, American painter/film maker
June Taylor, American dancer and choreographer

Politics/Military

George H. W. Bush, President of the United States
Hillary Rodham Clinton, First Lady, Senator, and Secretary
of State
Geraldine Ferraro, Congresswoman and Democratic
Candidate for Vice President
Edward Kennedy, U.S. Senator
Nita Lowey, Congresswoman
Sandra Day O'Connor, Justice of the U.S. Supreme Court
Ronald Reagan, President of the United States
Ann Richards, Governor of Texas

This section lists contemporaries whom the playwright may or may not have known]

Science

Elizabeth Arden, American cosmetologist
Virginia Apgar, American inventor of the Apgar Newborn
 Scoring System
Dr. Mary Ellen Avery, American neonatologist
Dr. Michael Drews, American fertility specialist
Robert Gallo, American biomedical researcher
Jane Goodall, English primatologist
Dr. Robert Guthrie, American neonatologist
Dr. James Speyer, American oncologist

Literature

Joseph Heller, American novelist
John Irving, American novelist
Michiko Kakutani, American literary critic
Stephen McCauley, American novelist
Toni Morrison, American novelist
V.S. Naipaul, Trinidadian-British novelist
Susan Sontag, American essayist
Muriel Spark, Scottish novelist
Tom Wolfe, American novelist and writer

Religion/Philosophy

Mortimer Adler, American philosopher
Hannah Arendt, German-American political theorist
Noam Chomsky, American philosopher
Hélène Cixous, French feminist
John Paul II, Pope
Gloria Steinem, American feminist
Elie Wiesel, Jewish theologian

Sports

Bonnie Blair, American speed skater
Chris Evert, American tennis player
Jackie Joyner-Kersee, American runner
Billie Jean King, American tennis champion

Greg Louganis, American Olympic diver
Martina Navratilova, Czech-American tennis player
Pete Sampras, American tennis player
Mark Spitz, American Olympic swimmer

Industry/Business

Martha Entenmann, Bakery entrepreneur
Roy Halston Frowick, American fashion designer
Bill Gates, American founder of Microsoft
Ruth Handler, American manufacturer of the Barbie Doll
Steve Jobs, American cofounder and CEO, of Apple, Inc.
Manuel "Manolo" Blahnik Rodriguez, Spanish founder of
 the shoe brand
Helena Rubinstein, Polish cosmetics industrialist
Bruce Wasserstein, American investment banker

WASSERSTEIN in an hour

A New Yorker Born and Bred

Wendy Joy Wasserstein was born in Brooklyn, New York, on October 18, 1950.

Her parents, Liska and Morris Wasserstein, had come to the United States from Poland as children, members of the "Great Migration" of persecuted Jews that took place between the World Wars. Liska Schleifer – better known as Lola – immigrated with her parents in 1928, when she was perhaps ten or eleven. Morris Wasserstein also came to the United States in 1928; he was six.

As a young woman, Lola met and married an up-and-coming businessman named George Wasserstein, and they had two children together, Sandra ("Sandy") and Abner. Then, shortly after George died of a ruptured appendix, Lola married George's youngest brother, Morris, and they had Georgette, Bruce and Wendy.

This first marriage, however, was kept hidden from the children of her second marriage until they were well into middle age. And Abner, who today would possibly be diagnosed as autistic, was hidden away in an institution, writes Wendy Wasserstein's biographer, Julie Salamon, in Wendy and the Lost Boys.

Not hidden was Lola and Morris's determination to succeed financially and socially in a country that offered education, freedom

---

This is the core of the book. The essay places the playwright in the context of his or her world and analyzes the influences and inspirations within that world.

from persecution and social mobility. Morris and his brothers had founded a ribbon-manufacturing company, which one day produced something that looked and felt a lot like velveteen. Lola pushed her children to be exceptional. They taught their children to be proud of being Jewish, but by no means were they strict, practicing Jews.

And so Wendy, like her sisters and her brother Bruce, attended private schools that generally stressed accomplishment and competition: Yeshiva of Flatbush, in Brooklyn; the Ethical Culture School; and the all-girls Calhoun School on Manhattan's Upper West Side, where Lola and Morris would frequently pick Wendy up in their cinnamon-colored Jaguar and drive her to their spacious home in Brooklyn.

At the end of Wendy's freshman year at Calhoun, Lola and Morris moved to a three-bedroom apartment on Manhattan's Upper East Side. The glittering city was now at Wendy's doorstep, and she was often the only Wasserstein child at home; her older siblings had decamped for careers and marriage, or (in Bruce's case) prep school.

Wendy had been named after the heroine of James M. Barrie's popular children's book, Peter Pan, and Manhattan became a kind of Never Never Land with which the adolescent Wendy fell in love. On Saturday mornings during the school year, Wendy took dancing lessons -- she aspired to be a ballerina -- and after class she often went with her mother to a Broadway matinee. She took taxis everywhere, shopped at Bergdorf's and other high-end Fifth Avenue department stores, and hung out with her classmates after school in their favorite Upper West Side restaurants.

She was falling in love with theater as well as with New York—one has the feeling that, while her friends were into the Beatles and Bob Dylan, Wendy was listening to musical comedies. But her practical theater experience seems to have been limited to acting in the occasional avant-garde production at Calhoun or working backstage. She did not spend her summers doing theater. A middling student, she spent two high-school summers taking remedial academic courses at Andover and Exeter, a couple of the Northeast's most elite prep schools.

Still, Wendy's teachers praised her imagination, if not her academic skills. The only person who did not praise Wendy was her mother, and that relationship would prove to have the most influence on Wasserstein's life and art.

Like Mother?

Lola, in various guises, is a running theme in Wasserstein's plays. In *Isn't It Romantic* (1983), for instance, she is easily identifiable as the character of Tasha Blumberg, a New York mother who laments that her daughter, Janie, is not married.

Lola is also a fixture in the many comical articles that Wasserstein wrote for mainstream magazines. With a combination of affection and irritation, Wasserstein wrote about how Lola used to barge to the front of the line at Radio City Music Hall, telling the usher that the family was visiting from Kansas and would be miserable if they did not get in to see Radio City. At Luchow's, a now defunct New York restaurant that was famous for enormous portions of German food, Lola frequently asked the Oompah band to serenade Wendy with "Happy Birthday" (even when it wasn't her birthday), so that her youngest daughter would overcome what Lola considered a crippling shyness.

By all accounts, Lola was impossible to ignore, for she always insisted on being the center of attention. She dressed and behaved flamboyantly; or as Wasserstein once wrote, "In an era personified by Donna Reed, my mother preferred Carmen Miranda." Lola was intrusive, less than motherly and skinny, an attribute that she always held over Wendy, who had a tendency to put on weight. After all, too much weight and Wendy would not be able to find a husband – marriage and children, in Lola's view, being the highest goals for a woman. "Your sister-in-law is pregnant," Wasserstein once quoted Lola as saying, "and that means more to me than a million dollars or any play."

The playwright Christopher Durang, who became a close friend of Wasserstein's at Yale Drama School, confided, "Wendy's portrayal of her mother in her plays tended to be way kinder than I thought her mother deserved. I thought Wendy would have been better served psychologically if she had gotten angrier in those plays." Indeed, at the end of *Isn't It Romantic* there's a kind of mother-daughter reconciliation, with each woman accepting the other's needs and differences.

But Wasserstein's ability to transform her mother into a character, and in that way gain a measure of control over her, came later in life. While growing up, she wrestled with Lola's contradictory messages. On the one hand, Lola applauded drive and aggression. On the other, she put a premium on a woman's physical attractiveness, and on marriage and motherhood. Which path should Wendy choose? Which path would win her mother's approval?

The attempt to resolve how a woman should live her life would dominate Wasserstein's plays. It was also a question on the minds of many young women of Wasserstein's generation.

Women's Lib

Wasserstein entered young womanhood when the country's second feminist wave, more popularly called Women's Liberation, was in full sway.

In 1960, the Food and Drug Administration (FDA) licensed the sale of the contraceptive pill, although in some states it was illegal for single women to receive and fill a prescription. But even with restrictions, the Pill, as it was referred to, gave women a new-found sexual freedom.

With sexual freedom came the freedom to delay marriage and motherhood, and pursue careers and financial independence. The term "Women's Liberation" consciously implied that women were oppressed by being confined to social and biological roles created by a dominant male society.

Liberation would help women break out, to define themselves, make their own choices about their bodies, and find careers in professions from which men had excluded them. "Consciousness-raising" groups sprang up all over the country, to help women share their experiences with other women, and turn women who felt fearful and oppressed into self-sufficient individuals.

Women's Liberation was largely a white middle-class movement during the 1960s and '70s, and some women embraced it more heartily than others. For many, the experience of hundreds of women marching together—exhorting each other to shed dependence and take control of their destiny—was exhilarating. For others, it aroused doubt and internal conflict.

The Uncommon Women *of Mount Holyoke*

In 1967, Wasserstein entered the all-women private college of Mount Holyoke, in South Hadley, Massachusetts.

As Salamon writes in Wendy and the Lost Boys, Wasserstein and many of her classmates were a trifle surprised to find that the college of their choice had not kept up with the times. If, as Bob Dylan wrote and sang in 1964, "The Times They Are a-Changin'"[3]Holyoke had apparently not noticed. Wasserstein and her friends "encountered a hothouse of girlieness," Salamon writes, "stuck in the 1950s, filled with bright women who seemed desperate to land a husband."

For Wasserstein, freshman year was particularly miserable— she nearly flunked out. She rebelled against the college's "land a husband" culture, with its emphasis on demure female behavior and its Friday exodus, when the campus emptied out as young women headed to their boyfriends' colleges for the weekend. In response, she ate too much, dressed sloppily and hung out with a crowd that consciously chose not to fit in. She did have a boyfriend—someone she had known since high school—but he seems to have wanted more emotional commitment than she was prepared to give.

Perhaps it was the experience of living with Lola and defending herself against Lola's critical jabs. Whatever the origin, Wasserstein had become an acute observer of character, possessed a sharp sense of humor and had a remarkably accurate memory for conversations.

The words and behavior of the young Holyoke women—the smart and daring ones whom she admired and sometimes envied, the ridiculous ones of whom she made fun, and the lonely and confused women (herself included)—would resurface in her break-out play, *Uncommon Women and Others* (1977). Holyoke, whatever its disappointments, would provide rich material for Wasserstein's writing, both in her plays and her essays.

Indirectly, Holyoke led Wasserstein to her career as a playwright. Wasserstein's major was history, but in her sophomore year, at a friend's suggestion, she took a drama course at nearby Smith College, and she wrote her first play: *Velveteen Goes to Taco Bell.*

The simple, farcical action was the kind that might have occurred on an episode of the television situation comedy "I Love Lucy," which Wasserstein had watched religiously while growing up. Salamon describes the plot in her biography: "a girl goes to a Taco Bell drive-in restaurant in California, gets torpedoed by five hundred burritos, and then eats her way out."

Len Berkman, who was in his first year of teaching at Smith and is now a full professor there, responded positively to the script's humor and boldness, although he also told Wasserstein that the play could never be staged, because no actor would be able to perform it night after night.

One suspects that Wasserstein, who had seen a great deal of theater by then, knew this and did not care. She was giving free rein to her comedic imagination and to an aggressive streak that flowed beneath her sometimes shy exterior, with its girlish, high-pitched voice and distinctive giggle. Berkman's class was possibly the most enjoyable academic experience of her college years. As she later said, "This was the first time I realized that a person could get credit in life for what they liked to do."

Marriage, Law School, Theater?

In *Uncommon Women and Others*, many of the female characters— students at a college for women obviously modeled on

Holyoke—reveal themselves to be confused about the best direction to take after they graduate.

Wasserstein was writing from both observation and personal experience: she graduated in spring 1971, uncertain about what to do next.

As always, Lola was there with a suggestion: marriage. But the only vaguely possible marital candidate was the young man Wasserstein had dated throughout college, and while he pined for her, she was not head-over-heels for him.

Job-hunting was not high on her agenda, either, and since she was still living at home and drawing on the Wasserstein family's affluence, supporting herself was not urgent. Law school, she believed, would please her mother, if marriage was not in the offing; she took, but failed, the law boards.

A theater friend whom she had met at college told her about a playwriting course at the venerable City College of New York (CCNY), and soon Wasserstein was trundling up to West 135th Street to take a workshop with the playwright Israel Horovitz and a creative writing class with Joseph Heller, who, ten years earlier, had become famous with the darkly comic novel *Catch-22*.

In both classes Wasserstein received encouragement for her writing, particularly her comic ability, although now and again a teacher would urge her to write with more emotional depth.

Armed with positive responses to her work, Wasserstein started sending short stories and comical essays to magazines and newspapers. But as nearly every freelance writer has experienced, breaking into the mainstream market is tough. Wasserstein collected rejections.

She also wrote a one-act play. Called *Any Woman Can't,* the title was a riff on psychiatrist David Reuben's patronizing but popular 1971 volume about women's sexual fulfillment, *Any Woman Can!* Courtesy of one of Lola's connections, *Any Woman Can't* made its way to Robert Moss, who had recently started a company called Playwrights Horizons dedicated to new work. Moss thought the script was humorous, although slight. But he met Wasserstein and liked her, and he scheduled the play for five performances in

April 1973.

Wasserstein may have started *Any Woman Can't* as a satiric response to Reuben's condescending attitudes, but she based her situations and characters on people she knew: her boyfriend and herself; her brother Bruce and his wife, Lynne. In the first relationship, the woman rejects the man—she says, outright, "I hate you"—and establishes an independent identity. In the second, the woman is subservient to the man in her life.

Wasserstein's friends and family were reportedly a little unnerved to see themselves represented so clearly. (Wasserstein's romance ended soon after her boyfriend saw the play, and Bruce's wife divorced him.) But for the playwright, this was a break-through. From then on, every major Wasserstein play would draw directly on personal experiences, her own and those of the people closest to her.

By the time Playwrights Horizons presented Any Woman Can't, Wasserstein had given the law boards a second try and passed. She applied for fall 1973 admission to both the Business School at Columbia University and the Yale School of Drama, and each accepted her. The first could conceivably send her on the kind of high-achieving, money-making path that her oldest sister and her brother were following. The second—well, who knows where that could lead?

She chose Yale.

Unhappy in New Haven

In 1924, Yale University had established a Department of Drama in its School of Fine Arts, and in 1955, the University set up the separate Yale School of Drama, a leading professional school for training actors, directors, designers, and playwrights.

By the 1960s, however, Yale School of Drama had lost ground as a cutting-edge institution, and so the University brought in the educator and theatre critic Robert Brustein to stir things up. Among other changes, he started Yale Repertory Theatre, so that the students could have a professional company with which to work.

Wasserstein went to Yale feeling optimistic. Respected American writers had spoken positively about her work; a play of hers had been produced, and audiences had enjoyed it. She had sent that script with her application to Yale.

But, ever Lola's daughter, at 23 she was more vulnerable to criticism than she anticipated, and more needy. And the Yale School of Drama was not in the business of coddling its students. After all, the world of the professional theater was a rough-and-tumble place. Yale Drama's administrators and faculty had favorites; Wasserstein was not one of them.

Indeed, she soon realized that, as at Holyoke, she did not fit in. Brustein had made a name as a critic by praising the European avant-garde; Wasserstein wrote light comedy. Making matters even more difficult, a fellow student staged a misguided production of *Any Woman Can't,* and Richard Gilman, Yale's other resident critical theorist, happened to see it. "I went to the production," Chris Durang recalls, "and I remembered that, when I had read the play, how much I had laughed. At this performance: no laughs. The main character was played rather seriously and really threw the play off. Afterward Gilman walked by Wendy and didn't say anything. And it felt like he wrote her off that day."

As at Holyoke, Wasserstein responded by dressing in rumpled fashion, letting her dark, curly hair go uncombed and eating too much.

But if the Drama School's faculty did not always appreciate Wasserstein, some of her fellow students did. She made friends at Yale, and Durang, who was in his third and final year when Wasserstein entered the program, was among the closest. "She was fun," Durang recalled. "She was very full of humor. I really enjoyed talking to her about theater, life, relationships. There was the sadness that [Salamon's] biography implies, but on a daily basis she had a real spark of enjoyment to her."

The two swapped stories about their off-kilter families, and Durang listened sympathetically to Wasserstein's tales of life with Lola. They showed each other the first drafts of their respective work. Clearly Wasserstein adored Durang, who was charming and talented, caring and considerate, but also gay and thus unavailable to Wasserstein romantically.

To Wasserstein's credit, she stuck it out at Yale. She wrote a one-act musical called *Montpelier Pa-zazz*. With Durang, who remained in New Haven the year after he graduated, from fall 1974 to spring 1975, she wrote a roughly 40-minute piece called *When Dinah Shore Ruled the Earth* for the Yale Cabaret. Her idea, according to Durang, arose from the Dewar's "White Label" print ads that highlighted people of achievement: the most recent book they had read, their latest accomplishment. "She had the idea for doing the Best Dewar's Award Ceremony," said Durang. "A kind of pageant. All the people had won the awards—they were all women of achievement—and I found it very funny, although it was kind of static. So I was advising her on it and after a certain point either I offered or she asked, 'Do you want to write this with me?' So I ended up adding well-known songs that one changed the lyrics to—contestants would have a short song -- and I ended up playing the MC."

As Durang remembers it, one character was a sexy Ann Margaret type. Another was a white woman who claimed she was a black militant lesbian. And the main figure, Holly, was a beautiful woman who had wonderful children and a marvelous husband. Unlike the Holly character, who would appear in *Uncommon Women and Others*, this Holly did not seem to be a stand-in for Wasserstein; she was played by someone small and blonde. "But the Holly figure did not have much confidence and was always trying to please everybody," said Durang. "Holly would say strange and vulnerable things in the midst of the others' strengths."

During that second year at Yale, Wasserstein also began to write scenes about her experiences at Holyoke, and she continued to work on this evolving play during her third and final year in New Haven. Her Yale colleagues did not always respond positively to the new work—long after Yale, Wasserstein would quote the chauvinist male playwright who commented, "I just can't get into all this chick stuff." But she did acquire admirers of her writing. The new play went up at Yale, and as with *Any Woman Can't*, audiences laughed and offered encouragement.

Brustein, however, did not, and almost alone among her fellow playwrights, Wasserstein received no accolades when she graduated Yale in spring 1976. She returned to New York uncertain of what to do next and without the self-confidence she had felt three years earlier. "In truth," Wasserstein wrote a friend from Holyoke, "I don't think I'm that good."

New Horizons

"When we're thirty we're going to be pretty f------g amazing."

That's Rita talking, in *Uncommon Women and Others*. As Wasserstein describes the character, "She refuses to live down to expectations. She shouldn't worry about it. Her imagination would never let her."

Lola might criticize her youngest daughter's looks or lack of a husband, but Lola also possessed grit, and this she had passed along to all her children, including Wendy. Somewhere in that post-Yale uncertainty the twenty-six-year-old Wasserstein knew she wanted to keep writing plays, and so she sent Montpelier Pa-zazz and her script for *Uncommon Women* to Bob Moss at Playwrights Horizons. Playwrights produced the first, and a man named André Bishop, who had more or less walked himself into the job of literary manager there, scheduled a workshop of *Uncommon Women* for March 1977. The two men liked Wasserstein personally and appreciated her writing, and they promised her a production of *Uncommon Women* down the road.

In the meantime, Wasserstein was hired to deliver scripts to the readers who would recommend plays for the esteemed National Playwrights Conference, which took place every summer at the Eugene O'Neill Theater Center in Waterford, Connecticut. Wasserstein cannily took advantage of the opportunity to deliver *Uncommon Women*, and in May 1977, Lloyd Richards, the Conference's artistic director, wrote Wasserstein that her script had been accepted.

In the United States in 1977 there was no other venue for developing new plays quite like "the O'Neill," as everyone referred to it. Situated on well-manicured grounds not far from the Sound, the O'Neill offered a cluster of run-down buildings and three outdoor playing spaces, where rehearsals and staged readings took place. Each playwright was assigned a director and a dramaturg, and during the day the playwright would discuss her script or rehearse, and at night she would return either to a nearby college dorm or (if lucky) to an actual house, where she would hunker down with her typewriter in a small room and pound out rewrites.

The morning after the second reading—usually a public reading—all the playwrights, dramaturgs, and directors would gather in one of the outdoor spaces, while Lloyd Richards led a tightly controlled discussion about the script.

For a playwright, the two months in the country could be an idyllic time. The accommodations were uncomfortable and the food not the best, but still, to live and talk the creation of new plays, communicate with a director and dramaturg dedicated to your work, and hang out with one's fellow dramatists, were luxuries. There is a photograph of Wasserstein at the O'Neill during that summer of 1977. She is sitting outdoors among a group, looking slim in a loose summer dress, flip-flops on her feet, her hair appealingly curly. But what is most striking is her demeanor. She looks relaxed, poised, and confident.

And well she might, for by all reports *Uncommon Women and Others* was the hit of the Conference. As staged by an up-and-coming director, Steven Robman, and with a cast skilled at working with new plays and performing script-in-hand, Wasserstein's play made colleagues and visiting audiences laugh and cry. Daniel Freudenberg, artistic director of the nonprofit Phoenix Theatre in New York City, attended a reading and offered Wasserstein a full production that autumn. She had promised the script to Bob Moss and André Bishop at Playwrights Horizons, but the Phoenix was a more established company, with a more impressive performance space (the proscenium stage at Marymount Manhattan College on East 71st Street). In Wasserstein's realistic assessment, her play would have a better cast and receive more attention from critics if the Phoenix produced it.

Her friends at Playwrights Horizons respected the decision, and on November 21, 1977, *Uncommon Women and Others* opened off Broadway at the Phoenix.

By Wendy Wasserstein

Uncommon Women and Others is a memory play. It begins with the brief voiceover of a man describing the superior qualities of the women whom "the college" produces and then shifts to a scene at a New York restaurant, where five friends who graduated six years earlier are reuniting over lunch. They playfully reenact the college dining-room ritual of clinking their glasses with silverware, to get everyone's attention, and with that gesture the action shifts to the college itself, where these same women are seniors, wrestling daily with the most important decision of their lives: what to do after college.

Wasserstein had labored over how to structure the play and the result is two acts containing episodic scenes, mostly set at the women's college and introduced by the male voice over. In the final episode, however, the man's voice dissolves, a woman's voice takes up the narration, and once again we see these women at the restaurant, six years older and still struggling with the question of what to do with their lives.

The structure supports the play's strongest elements – elements that would become Wasserstein's signature as a playwright: the characters and the humor. "I find that when the character work is good," Wasserstein once said in an interview with this writer, "then things become funny. For myself, I find it harder to say, 'Oh, I'm going to be funny, and this will be my vessel,' than to show what particular characters do . . . My writing comes from that school of women writers —Clare Boothe Luce, Anita Loos, Edna Ferber—who wrote witty women . . . basically the women whom I write are witty people, and they're witty and funny for a reason, whether they're deflecting, whether they're trying to puncture male pretentiousness, whether this is how they get by in society. These people happen to be funny or witty or ironic for a reason. Line for line, it scales as funny, but it actually has to do with character."

Based undoubtedly on women whom Wasserstein had known at school, the characters are recognizable types but authentic—we see ourselves in them. There is Kate (Jill Eikenberry), the self-directed but scared young woman who wants a serious career, and there is Samantha (Ann McDonough), who (much like Wasserstein's older sister Georgette) is beautiful and wants only to be married and have a family. Rita (Swoosie Kurtz) is the adventuresome one who likes to shock everybody with her behavior, and Muffet (Ellen Parker) is confused about whether to be a feminist or not. Holly Kaplan (Alma Cuervo)—the lone Jewish girl in this mix and the character most clearly based on Wasserstein—is overweight, without a boyfriend, and feels lonely and isolated. And there are several secondary characters, including the annoyingly chipper Susie Friend (Cynthia Herman)—the perfect girl everybody loves to hate—and the anxious academic achiever, Leilah (Glenn Close).

Ultimately, though, the play's cleverness lies in the structure. Throughout most of *Uncommon Women,* Wasserstein entertains us with glimpses of these vibrant young women, each smart in her own way, each verbal and witty. Surely, we think, as we see them hanging out in their dorm discussing men, class work, and life, any self-doubt will be temporary and they will all have magnificent, uncommon destinies.

But in the final scene Wasserstein delivers the punch. Even though a couple of the friends attain the destinies they intended, none of them are satisfied or truly happy, Holly Kaplan especially. Quite the opposite: uncommon still, they are even more conflicted than when they were at school.

The reviews were generally effusive, and as Wasserstein had hoped, significant New York City and national publications weighed in. Almost every mainstream critic praised Robman's direction and the cast, and welcomed a new, young voice to the American theater. Richard Eder, reviewing for The New York Times, wrote that "A terror of choices and the future afflicts all of [these women], and Miss Wasserstein has made this anguish most movingly real, amid all the jokes and the knowing sophistication." Marilyn Stasio in *Cue* magazine called it "Hilarious, touching, witty, insightful, and a lot of other nice things." Edith Oliver, who knew the play from the O'Neill, where she was a regular dramaturg, wrote in *The New Yorker* about the "wonderful, original comedy. It is the girls and the games they play and their conversations that make the show, and every moment is theatrical. 'We are all allowed one dominant characteristic,' somebody says. That is not entirely true. The characters are never allowed to become types, and, for all their funny talk and behavior, they are sympathetically drawn."

Even the notoriously tough John Simon praised Wasserstein for "a chortlingly mischievous sense of outer and inner dialogue, of what these collegians said or merely thought; and she observes her characters, one of whom must be herself, with a nice blend of sympathy and unsentimentality." But he also urged Wasserstein to reach for a larger canvas. "There is no shape, no sense of direction, no purpose here, except recording something for memory's sake, which is all too private a pursuit."

Indeed, not everyone jumped on the bandwagon. *Time* magazine's Ted Kalem wrote, "While the play is laced with affectionately bantering humor and a gamy ration of powder-room candor, the characters are stereotypical." The feminist critic Helene Keyssar would later describe the characters as "embarrassing stereotypes of female college students" and complain that Wasserstein had offered no alternative to, or substantial criticism of, her characters' restrictive world.

Both objections—that her characters were stereotypical and that she was soft on feminism—would follow Wasserstein throughout her career. But for the moment, *Uncommon Women and Others* was an Off-Broadway hit, and the amount of ink spent discussing it was bringing the twenty-seven-year-old dramatist a national reputation. The production sold out its entire short run (it closed on December 22, 1977, because the Phoenix had another show scheduled). Soon, however, Channel Thirteen/WNET filmed the play for *Great Performances: Theater in America.* In May 1978, with the original cast except for Close, who was replaced by

Meryl Streep, Wasserstein's images of educated but self-doubting American women traveled into living rooms across the nation and made the young playwright a legion of fans.

Family Drama

In the publishing world, it is well-known that second novels are difficult to write if one has had tremendous success with the first major work. And so it was with Wasserstein as she sought to find a subject and a form for her next play.

Her professional and personal lives had grown more complex since the success of *Uncommon Women*. She had acquired a good agent and was receiving film and television assignments, although few scripts actually were shot. She moved deeper into the New York theater world and had a love affair with a notable Broadway lyricist.

But some things never change. Lola and Morris were proud of their daughter's accomplishment, if taken aback by the image of the distressed Holly/Wendy in the play. But Lola was still kibitzing from the sidelines, wondering why her daughter was nearly thirty and single. What good were applause and rave reviews if Wendy was living in an apartment by herself, with no husband or children? So when Steven Robman, now the Phoenix Theatre's artistic director, commissioned Wasserstein in 1979 to write a new play, she wrote about a young woman's relationship with her parents and the need to get away from an overbearing mother.

Family plays, particularly serious dramas, have traditionally been the American playwright's strong suit. Eugene O'Neill's *Long Day's Journey into Night,* Tennessee Williams's *The Glass Menagerie*, Arthur Miller's *Death of a Salesman*—the American theater's greatest plays have focused on the conflicts between a family's older and younger generations. In a sense *Uncommon Women and Others* is a family play, although not in a conventional way. The young women form a kind of family at college and are trying to recapture that community years after they graduate.

Isn't It Romantic involves a daughter trying to separate herself from her parents and live her own life, a premise that is traditional in one sense—there's a generational conflict—and unconventional in another: until the 1970s, most American family plays were about young men clashing with their parents, particularly their fathers. But Wasserstein had no use for that convention. Here is Janie Blumberg, the central character of *Isn't It Romantic*, a short, plump would-be writer who is trying to navigate between the only choices that seem available to her: the supposed safety of the controlling doctor who wants to marry her, as her mother strongly recommends, and the lonely independence that her elegant friend Harriet recommends—until somebody wants to marry Harriet, who quickly dumps her principles.

As in *Uncommon Women*, Janie is caught between society's expectations of how a woman should behave and her desire to be her own person. But perhaps unlike Wasserstein in real life, Janie manages to stand up to her parents, who prove understanding and accepting. At the end of the play Janie is alone in her new apartment, dancing by herself. She has spurned the man whom she did not truly want and has been betrayed, as she experiences it, by her female friend. But she is apparently at peace with her decision.

The Phoenix production did not go smoothly. In 1984, for an interview with the Times' Michiko Kakutani, Wasserstein said that at one point during the first week of performances she had Janie (Alma Cuervo) deciding to marry the doctor (Peter Riegert). Wasserstein's script probably would have benefited from the extensive readings and workshops that *Uncommon Women* had received. As it was, the "development" took place during rehearsals, an old-fashioned method but one not ideally suited to Wasserstein's process. "I write pretty slowly," she once told the scholar David Savran. "Once I'm writing I'm okay, but I rewrite a great deal. And sometimes my plays seem too well crafted. They're too well written, so they seem easier than they are. They're actually quite difficult to write. To get that kind of smoothness takes a lot of writing."

Directed by Robman, *Isn't It Romantic* opened on May 28, 1981. Mel Gussow wrote a mixed review in The New York Times.

"Miss Wasserstein seems a bit unsure what she wants," he wrote. "Her play . . . veers from character comedy to caricature, interspersed with throwaway jokes and routines, but there is no denying the playwright's comic virtuosity and her ear for contemporary jargon." But his colleague, Walter Kerr, who wrote criticism for the Times' Sunday edition, was less even-handed. Along with patronizing references to "feminine sensibility" and "the girls" (Kerr apparently had no patience for feminism), he skewered Wasserstein with the unkindest cut of all. "The one thing I'm not sure of," he wrote, "is whether Miss Wasserstein is in any special sense a dramatist."

Some playwrights don't read reviews, but Wasserstein read that one and was understandably distressed. As Salamon suggests in her biography, the anxiety Wasserstein had experienced at Yale came rushing back, only partially alleviated by new accomplishments: a Guggenheim fellowship; teaming up with Christopher Durang to adapt a *New Yorker* short story into a film (*House of Husbands*). Ensemble Studio Theatre produced a delicate one-act called Tender Offer, in which a tired businessman picks his nine-year-old daughter up at a dance studio, after missing her recital, and father and daughter talk, share feelings, and then dance. Readers were responding warmly to the amusing, lightly personal essays she had begun writing for magazines, and her friendships with André Bishop, now artistic director of Playwrights Horizons, and an imaginative young director named Gerald Gutierrez, grew deeper.

But as always with Wasserstein, drive existed side-by-side with self-questioning, and during the summer of 1983 she and Gutierrez began to work on *Isn't It Romantic* in preparation for a new production at Playwrights Horizons. That production opened on December 15, 1983, with a new cast, fresh design team, and a script that reviewers agreed was more consistent in tone and more focused than the one presented prematurely at the Phoenix. At the Times, Mel Gussow wrote that "In her new, improved version of *Isn't It Romantic*, Wendy Wasserstein has added a sweet humanity to her comic cautionary tale about a young woman's ascent to adulthood." The *Variety* critic wrote, "If Dorothy Parker were a playwright today, she might have written this endearingly acid comedy." Edith Oliver of *The New Yorker* called Wasserstein "among the funniest and most inventive writers around."

This play about a young, middle-class New York woman trying to juggle obligations to family and self touched audiences, who made the show a hit. Playwrights moved the production to the Lucille Lortel Theatre for an open commercial run. There it racked up 733 performances, providing Wasserstein with royalties on which she could live (a rare event in the theater). The play's humor and humanity made it equally successful at regional theaters.

Playwrights Horizons had kept Wasserstein's playwriting career on track by generously offering her a chance to rewrite her script and see it produced again soon after its first, mediocre outing. André Bishop believed in Wasserstein's talent, cared for her enormously, and wanted her in the Playwrights Horizons fold. Wasserstein returned the favor by making the company her theatrical home.

The Ascendance of Women Who Write Plays

On Sunday, May 1, 1983, *The New York Times Magazine* carried an article by theater critic Mel Gussow called "Women Playwrights: New Voices in the Theater." Although Gussow featured Marsha Norman, who had recently won the Pulitzer Prize for Drama for *'Night, Mother*, he included the thirty-two-year-old Wasserstein in his comments about female playwrights worthy of notice.

American women had been making inroads in American theater since the 1960s, when playwrights including Maria Irene Fornes, Adrienne Kennedy, and Megan Terry began to be produced Off-Off Broadway. During the 1970s, the Women's Liberation Movement had spurred women to form their own theater companies, and many women around the country established alternative theaters that were communal, noncommercial, and dedicated to feminist content. At the same time, emerging groups such as The Women's Project and regional theaters like Actors Theatre of Louisville were bringing female playwrights into the mainstream. Beth Henley's *Crimes of the Heart* was originally produced at Actors Theatre, and Henley went on to win the Pulitzer in 1981when it was produced in New York—the first woman to win this award since 1956. The Susan Smith Blackburn Prize, established in 1978, was being awarded to women only; *Uncommon Women* had been a finalist in 1979 and *Isn't It Romantic* in 1981.

Ironically, by the time Gussow and the *New York Times* looked around and saw what was happening, a number of women's theater companies were folding, and the Women's Movement was struggling. The second wave of American feminism, which had flourished alongside the sexual revolution of the 1960s and the movement to stop the Vietnam War, ran up against a neo-conservative counter-revolution. Ronald Reagan, who had been elected President of the United States in 1981 and would hold office until 1989, would preside over a decade that saw the strengthening of American religious fundamentalism, with its public denigration of feminists and praise for traditional female roles.

Women who wrote plays would continue to enter the American theater in significant numbers, but the number of plays by women that were produced did not keep pace. And many women who had liberated themselves in the 1960s and '70s saw that they had not succeeded in changing American society—or themselves—to the extent they had hoped.

It is likely that Wasserstein, with her keen observations of society, had discerned the changing spirit of the times when rewriting *Isn't It Romantic*. But she was still engrossed in exploring her family as a topic and turned her attention to a musical called *Miami*, which she had been working on with the songwriters Jack Feldman and Bruce Sussman.

Inspired by the Christmas vacations Wasserstein had spent with her family in Miami, when she was a child, the musical was partly about Wasserstein's relationship with her brother Bruce and partly about Belle Barth, a raunchy comedian who used to play the nightclubs of Miami Beach (influencing Bette Midler, among others). Feldman and Sussman wanted to focus on Barth, since she was clearly a theatrical character; Wasserstein was more interested in the family story. Gerald Gutierrez, who directed a sold-out workshop at Playwrights Horizons in January 1986, could not resolve the differences to anyone's satisfaction. To Wasserstein's deep disappointment, the project died. Other than that presentation, open to the public but not to the press, *Miami* was not produced in her lifetime.

In addition to writing about the family in which she had grown up, Wasserstein, now thirty-five, was trying to establish one of her own. Her friendship with André Bishop of Playwrights Horizons had become a platonic love affair. They were close enough, according to Salamon's biography, to circle around the question of marriage, although Bishop was gay and believed that marriage would be an unfair arrangement for both of them. Also, Wasserstein wanted children, and Bishop was not ready to be a parent.

The affair ended, leaving Wasserstein feeling alone, adrift and perhaps a bit angry. Not only was her personal world unmoored, but also the world around her was changing in threatening ways. The feminist solidarity that Wasserstein had experienced at Holyoke seemed far in the past; in the present, the Women's Movement was unraveling; a result of right-wing onslaughts, middle-class Women's Libbers now chasing personal success, and the lack of a sense of urgency. And in the theater and beyond, a mysterious disease called AIDS was attacking and killing gay men, decimating the theater family. Many of Wasserstein's friends would die.

The affair with Bishop was over, but the professional relationship continued. He commissioned a new play from Wasserstein, and in 1987, in a spurt of passionate creativity, she wrote *The Heidi Chronicles*.

Chronicling Women's Times

Watching *The Heidi Chronicles* onstage is like watching a history of the Women's Liberation Movement. The play is not only the personal chronicle of Heidi Holland, an attractive, single, slightly caustic forty-year-old art history professor; it is also a sometimes satiric, sometimes mournful chronicle of feminist times, as Wasserstein experienced them.

The action begins in 1989, with Heidi giving a lecture about female painters at Columbia University. The scene then shifts to 1965, when Heidi is sixteen and at a high-school dance, where she meets a boy named Peter Patrone, who may turn out to be the love of her life. From there the action moves forward in time, as Heidi grows to womanhood. She stumps in New Hampshire for aspiring Presidential candidate Eugene McCarthy and has an affair with an aggressive young journalist. She warily attends a women's conscious-raising session but enthusiastically protests the sexist practices of a Chicago museum. Her journalist lover marries someone else, and her high-school friend, who has become a doctor, is gay in the age of AIDS.

Heidi travels from optimism to disillusionment. But the disillusion is not so much with the men in her life as it is with a movement that she believes has failed the intelligent, principled women of her generation. In one of the play's frequently cited scenes, set in 1986 at New York City's Plaza Hotel, Heidi gives a speech to her prep school alumnae. She is supposed to talk about "Women, Where Are We Going?" Instead, she describes being in the locker room of her gym and how isolated she felt in relation to the competitive, self-involved women around her. "I'm just not happy," she says to the aerobics teacher. "I'm afraid I haven't been happy for some time." In closing, she tells her fellow alums: "It's just that I feel stranded. And I thought the whole point was that we wouldn't feel stranded. I thought the point was that we were all in this together."

Two scenes later, it is 1989 again and Heidi is in an empty room in a new apartment, much like Janie Blumberg at the end of *Isn't It Romantic*. But where Janie repudiated her family and boyfriend to strike out on her own, Heidi has searched for community and, as she sees it, come up empty. So, on the eve of the twentieth century's final decade, she has started her own family, vowing that the adopted daughter she cradles will be "a heroine for the twenty-first."

Playwrights Horizons produced the play in a workshop at the Seattle Repertory Theatre, where it opened under Dan Sullivan's direction on April 6, 1988, away from the eyes of the New York press. Sullivan also staged the production that opened at Playwrights Horizons on December 12, 1988. Slim, blonde Joan Allen, who had won the Tony Award ® for Best Actress the previous spring in Lanford Wilson's *Burn This* played Heidi, and the rest of the fine cast included Boyd Gaines as Peter Patrone, Peter Friedman as the journalist Scoop Rosenbaum, and Ellen Parker, Drew McVety, Anne Lang, Joanne Camp, and Sarah Jessica Parker. On March 9, 1989, the Schubert Organization in association with Playwrights opened *The Heidi Chronicles* at the Plymouth Theatre, with Cynthia Nixon replacing Sarah Jessica Parker.

Wendy Wasserstein Had Arrived on Broadway.

"All people deserve to fulfill their potential."
—Heidi Holland in *The Heidi Chronicles*

The mainstream press generally applauded what they perceived to be the work of a significant and maturing playwright. Mel Gussow, reviewing the Playwrights Horizons production for the *New York Times*, wrote, "With her ambitious new play, [Ms. Wasserstein] both broadens and intensifies her beam, to give us a group picture over decades, a picture of women who want it all - motherhood, sisterhood, love and boardroom respect." He added approvingly, "Ms. Wasserstein has always been a clever writer of comedy. This time she has been exceedingly watchful about not settling for easy laughter, and the result is a more penetrating play. This is not to suggest, however, that *The Heidi Chronicles* is ever lacking in humor."

Linda Winer, chief theater critic for Newsday, was more effusive. "[*The Heidi Chronicles*]," she wrote, "is a wonderful and important play. Smart, compassionate, witty, courageous, this one not only dares to ask the hard questions . . . but asks them with humor, exquisite clarity and great fullness of heart." Howard Kissel of the *Daily News* told readers that "This is not just a funny play, but a wise one."

Awards poured in. The New York Drama Critics Circle voted *The Heidi Chronicles* the best play of the 1988-89 season. It won the Tony Award ® for Best Play, the Drama Desk Award for Best Play, the Susan Smith Blackburn Prize, and that most coveted recognition, the Pulitzer Prize for Drama. Wasserstein was the third female playwright in the 1980s, along with Marsha Norman and Beth Henley, to win the Pulitzer, and the ninth woman to win the prize since it was first awarded in 1918.

There were naysayers. William A. Henry III at *Time* magazine wrote that the "play is more documentary than drama, evoking fictionally all the right times and places but rarely attaining much thorny particularity about the people who inhabit them." John Simon, in *New York* magazine, wrote that the play was "ultimately unsatisfying" and that theatergoers wanted more from Wasserstein than "this mixture of parlor feminism and untrue confessions." (He later confessed to appreciating the Broadway incarnation more than the Off-Broadway one).

Among feminist critics, some cheered that a woman's play had reached Broadway and won the Pulitzer, others protested that Wasserstein's visibility was leading her to be anointed a spokesperson for her generation. Wasserstein, these critics wrote, had done a disservice to the Women's Movement with her satire (the amusing consciousness-raising scene portrays feminists as silly and rigid) and her regressive message. From their point of view, the playwright was saying that a woman, even one with a solid career, could only be happy if she was a mother. The radical feminist critic Gayle Austin wrote, "The trouble with this play is that although it raises issues, Wasserstein undercuts serious consideration through facile supporting female characters, sit-com humor, and a passive heroine who forms an absence at the center of the play."

Wasserstein chose to avoid the controversy. "Why call it feminist?" she asked Cathleen Stinson Ouderkirk during an interview for the *Christian Science Monitor (*Oct. 10, 1989). 'You'd never ask a man 'Is this a masculinist play?' I didn't write it as either a feminist tract or a non-feminist tract. I wasn't setting out to be didactic in any way. "To me," she continued, "good playwriting is about a character, not a political philosophy. 'Heidi' is about an art historian who goes through a sad period in her life and comes out of it. It's just a play about a girl, a character. If there's an idea, it comes from her."

That last statement was either naïve or simply Wasserstein dodging the issue, because obviously a character's ideas come originally from the dramatist. Ultimately, as Wasserstein well understood, the more controversy, the more people buy tickets.

But as was always the case with the best of Wasserstein's plays, audiences left the critics far behind. Theatergoers saw their own experiences in the characters and situations she created; they trooped to the Plymouth Theater, and laughed and cried at *The Heidi Chronicles* for 622 performances.

Sisters Three

The 1990s opened with Wasserstein at the highest point in her career. Not only was she a successful commercial playwright—a rarity in the theater for a man or a woman—she was writing prolifically for magazines and newspapers, was being interviewed in all the media, and she was traveling around the country, speaking to college students and teachers about what it meant to be a woman and a playwright.

Friends and relatives were often amazed by the number of people who came up to Wasserstein on the street or in restaurants to say hello, whether they knew her or not. But of course they did know her; they had been reading her personal essays for years. They knew about her search for the perfect man, they knew about her difficulties with Lola. They knew that when Wasserstein won the Pulitzer, Lola immediately started telling friends it was the Nobel Prize, as if the Pulitzer wasn't good enough. They knew and they empathized.

In *The Heidi Chronicles*, Heidi is looking for companionship and support, or as Wasserstein told Ouderkirk, "People need to connect sometime. You don't want to be outside all of your life. You want to land; you want to have a home of some sort." Failing to find a home in the Women's Movement or with the men she encounters, Heidi creates her own home. Wasserstein, now in her forties, began to explore her options for starting a family.

First, however, she returned thematically to the family in which she had grown up, particularly her older sisters Sandra and Georgette, and wrote her second Broadway hit, *The Sisters Rosensweig*. After a workshop at the Seattle Repertory Theatre, the play traveled back to New York to be produced in the Mitzi E. Newhouse Theatre at Lincoln Center, where André Bishop had become artistic director in January 1992. It opened there on October 22, 1992, staged by Daniel Sullivan, who had guided *The Heidi Chronicles*, and starred Jane Alexander, Frances McDormand, and Madeline Kahn. On March 18, 1993, with Christine Estabrook replacing McDormand, the production opened on Broadway at the Barrymore Theatre.

Alexander, McDormand and Kahn played three Jewish, Brooklyn-born sisters who reunite in London to celebrate the fifty-fourth birthday of the oldest, the high-achieving banker Sara Goode (Alexander). Gorgeous Teitelbaum (Kahn), the middle sister, is a wife, mother and wonderfully noisy radio personality, and Pfeni (McDormand), the youngest, better known as Penny, is a journalist who roams the world and has an aversion to settling down.

Like the female characters in Wasserstein's previous plays, the women generally find the men in their lives (Richard Klein, John Vickery) to be disappointing. But unlike in *Isn't It Romantic* or *The Heidi Chronicles*, these women turn out to be good at bonding with each other, possibly because they are family, possibly because they truly like each other. They mother each other, and the only actual mother-daughter relationship involves Sara and Tess (Julie Dretzin), who tussle quietly about Tess's desire to join a revolution in Vilnius with her Catholic boyfriend (Patrick Fitzgerald).

There is much hilarity, largely because Gorgeous is a tremendously funny part. Wasserstein ultimately edited the role after the first performance, because the comic potency of Madeline Kahn as Gorgeous distracted from the rest of the script.

"[*The Sisters Rosensweig*] is a well-made boulevard comedy," said Wasserstein, "but it starred two comic geniuses, Madeline Kahn and Robert Klein. So we go to the first preview of this play, and Madeline is so funny that when she goes off stage, you lose the through-line of the play, which is about Jewish identity, American identity. A woman lights the Sabbath candle, her sister blows it out, somebody's had a hysterectomy. All sorts of stuff going on there. From the audience you'd hear cough, cough, cough. So afterward, Dan [Sullivan] took me out and said, 'We're going to have to look at the story you're trying to tell, and you're going to have to cut some of Dr. Gorgeous, because when it's too funny, you've got a problem. You've got almost hysteria, and then the play just drops.'

"I've noticed that with my plays, because the comic characters, which I write best—are the more vivid supporting roles. They're larger, they're funnier. And the through-line character—he Heidi, the observer, Sara Goode in *The Sisters Rosensweig*—they're a beige color. So what happens is, the brighter comedy, the people in red with the bright red hair, the people that make me laugh, too—can change the shape of the show."

Kahn still stole the show, but the play, under Sullivan's guidance and Wasserstein's determined rewrites, became a tight, balanced mingling of humor and pathos. "*The Sisters Rosensweig* is Wendy Wasserstein's captivating look at three *Uncommon Women* and their quest for love, self-definition and fulfillment," wrote Mel Gussow in the *New York Times*. Shortly after the Broadway opening, Wasserstein received the William Inge Award for Distinguished Achievement in American Theatre. *The Sisters Rosensweig* was nominated for a Tony Award ® for Best Play, although the award that season went to Tony Kushner's epic *Angels in America: Millennium Approaches*. Kahn, however, won the Tony Award ® for Best Actress in a Play, and Wasserstein's latest hit ran for 556 performances.

American Daughters

The 1990s were a confusing period in the history of the United

States. The decade opened with a war in the Middle East—the first Gulf War—and ended with the President of the United States, William Jefferson Clinton, impeached by the House of Representatives. Along the way, while some issues of concern to women triumphed, others were met with defeat. The presence of Hillary Clinton as First Lady felt at first like a victory for the long-ago Women's Movement out of which Mrs. Clinton had emerged, a bright, aggressive graduate of a women's college setting out to change the world. Watching her stand by the man who had humiliated her with a back-stairs affair and then lied about it came as a blow.

For Wasserstein personally the decade was full of contrasts. During the Seattle workshop of *The Sisters Rosensweig*, she had learned that her sister Sandra was suffering from a recurrence of breast cancer. Wasserstein herself was going forward with attempts to become pregnant, as determined to have a baby as Sandra was to survive. Neither was having much success.

She worked hard: a television movie of *The Heidi Chronicles* starring Jamie Lee Curtis (1995); a children's book called *Pamela's First Musical* (1996); *The Object of My Affection,* a screenplay she adapted from Stephen McCauley's novel of the same title, about the friendship between a gay man and a pregnant social worker (1997); articles for *The New Yorker* magazine and the new on-line magazine *Slate*; and a short opera called *Festival of Regrets*—with music composed by Deborah Drattell—part of the Central Park trilogy at Glimmerglass Opera in Cooperstown, New York (1999).

She socialized intensely, rarely saying no to the opportunity to speak on a panel or appear at a benefit. In 1995, the Theatre Development Fund invited her to participate in its Open Doors program. For one year she took eight public-high-school students to the theater, introducing them to plays and discussing what they had seen over pizza after the show. She felt it was one of the most rewarding experiences of her career.

An American Daughter, which was first produced in June 1996 as a workshop at the Seattle Repertory Theatre, reflects the decade's confusion and Wasserstein's anger with the state of the nation. Set in Washington, D.C., the action involves a forty-two-year-old doctor and Senator's daughter, Lyssa Dent Hughes (Meryl Streep in Seattle, Kate Nelligan in New York), who has been nominated to be Surgeon General. Unfortunately, Hughes's past includes misplacing a jury summons, and a television reporter seizes on this accidental misstep to derail the nomination.

More intensely satirical than her previous plays, *An American Daughter* takes on political hypocrisy, the absurdity and the destructiveness of the media, and husbands who betray their wives. It is also more sprawling than any of Wasserstein's previous plays, as though she had more to say about the country's shortcomings than she could fit within a neatly structured boulevard comedy; she is making a conscious effort to broaden her scope and integrate family drama with public issues.

Lincoln Center Theater took the play directly to Broadway, where it opened at the Cort Theatre on April 13, 1997. But André Bishop's faith in the script was not echoed in the mainstream reviews, led by Ben Brantley's for The New York Times. He essentially complained that Wasserstein was taking on too much at once and oversimplifying as a result. "Ms. Wasserstein," Brantley wrote, "may be saying something about a world that reduces people to sound bites and social abstractions . . . . Yet the playwright is also working principally in bite-size slices of sound, sentiment and humor. When a character comes forth with a line like ''I don't know who I'm supposed to be anymore," it never feels truly earned by what came before . . . . The dazzling Ms. Nelligan, an expert in portraying conflicted souls, is wasted in an idealized, passive role that seems little more than a poster for Ms. Wasserstein's feelings about a country that continues to thwart its best and brightest women."

Feminist critics were more positive, appreciating what Wasserstein was trying to do rather than condemning her for not completely achieving it.

But reviews, good or bad, were probably not on Wasserstein's mind. Sandra's cancer had advanced, and two days after the opening the playwright flew to London for her frail sister's sixtieth birthday.

Seven months later, on December 30, 1997, Sandra died in New York.

But just as Wasserstein lost her sister, she found her daughter. By the time Sandra died, Wasserstein had largely given up on her attempts to become pregnant. But a chance encounter with the physician she had been consulting for fertility treatments led to a last try at in-vitro fertilization, and in spring 1999, at the age of forty-eight, she became pregnant. She told only a few people—Lola not among them—and on September 12, 1999, Lucy Jane Wasserstein came into the world, prematurely and by caesarean section. After many edgy weeks when no one was sure the baby would survive, Lucy Jane's Wasserstein tenacity kicked in, and shortly before Thanksgiving she went home with her mother.

Like Heidi, Wasserstein had created her own family.

Final Act

Life with Lucy Jane was delightful but also hectic. Ensconced with her daughter in a new apartment on Central Park West, Wasserstein oversaw a team that included a nanny and sometimes two assistants. Concerned about making money, according to Salamon's biography, Wasserstein worked feverishly: movie scripts; speaking engagements; and the December 2000 production of her newest play, *Old Money*, at Lincoln Center Theater.

She had tapped her family's personalities for all of her major plays, beginning with herself in *Uncommon Women and Others*. But she had never successfully dramatized her brother Bruce, who had transformed from a politically liberal do-gooder in college to a billionaire and out-and-out capitalist. *Old Money*, which Wasserstein had largely written while pregnant, was an attempt to expose the new Jewish rich, represented in the play by the hedge fund analyst Jeffrey Bernstein (Mark Harelik), and tie them thematically to the robber barons that stole from the poor and gave to themselves one hundred years earlier. The play, set in a New York City mansion, shifts back and forth in time.

41

Perhaps her personal life interfered with Wasserstein's ability to work through the play's structural and thematic problems, although she would have been the first to disagree. Possibly the script simply needed workshops and time. By comparison with her previous plays, *Old Money* was long on ideas but short on character development—an unusual occurrence in a Wasserstein script.

In any event, the play opened at the Mitzi E. Newhouse on December 7, 2000, directed by Mark Brokaw, who had staged Paula Vogel's Pulitzer Prize-winning drama, *How I Learned to Drive* (Daniel Sullivan had been offered Wasserstein's script but turned it down). *Old Money* received largely negative reviews and closed on January 21, 2001.

Once again Wasserstein embarked on a round of projects, including a publicity tour for *Shiksa Goddess*, a collection of her articles and essays. But it all proved too much for her health. Previously, she rushed energetically from event to event, airport to airport; now she was often exhausted and suffered frequently from dizziness. In addition she was diagnosed with Bell's palsy—nerve damage that causes facial paralysis. She would seem to recover from the paralysis, but then the palsy would recur. Her health continued to deteriorate. Still, she mustered energy to send a proposal for a novel, *Elements of Style*, to her editor at Knopf (it would be published after her death); worked with the composer Cy Coleman on an adaptation of *Pamela's First Musical*; and wrote several one-acts, among them a one-act script called *Third,* which Daniel Sullivan urged her to expand into a full-length play.

The opening scene of Third initially calls to mind *The Heidi Chronicles*; the play begins with an English professor, Laurie Jameson, giving a lecture to her class about Shakespeare's *King Lear*. A feminist, Jameson believes that "Cordelia is the traditional feminine victim, and therefore traditionally regarded as the heroine of the play." She describes Goneril and Regan, usually considered Cordelia's malevolent sisters, as "the girls with guts.

But structurally, *Third* bears no resemblance to *The Heidi Chronicles*. The action is very much in the present. Having established Jameson's feminist credentials, Wasserstein then proceeds to demonstrate how ideology can cloud judgment. Jameson accuses a student, one Woodson Bull III, known as "Third," of plagiarizing his *Lear* paper. It is too fine, she believes, for someone who is majoring in sociology, wants to be a sports agent, and she assumes, hails from a conservative background. She brings him up on charges, loses, and reevaluates her behavior and her principles.

The basic plot—the teacher who is taught a lesson—is as old as drama itself. But the scenes between Jameson and Third are lively and play well. Scenes between Jameson and her senile father are poignant, as is the interaction between the professor and her closest friend, a female colleague battling cancer. The parallels with King Lear are a bit obvious, but the image of a middle-aged woman trying to deal with what life throws at her—an aging parent, a smart and rebellious daughter, challenges to an ideology on which she staked her career—compels our attention.

Directed by Daniel Sullivan, *Third* opened at the Mitzi E.Newhouse Theater at Lincoln Center on October 24, 2005, six days after Wasserstein's fifty-fifth birthday. The reviews were mixed for the play, ecstatic for the performances, particularly Dianne Wiest as Professor Jameson and Charles Durning in the role of her father. But as with Wassserstein's earliest plays, it really didn't matter what the critics wrote. Lincoln Center Theater's subscribers flocked to the production.

By opening night, Wasserstein was so ill she could barely walk. She wore braces on her legs, and at home there was a nurse to bathe and dress her, and help her into bed at night. A conventional wheelchair would have announced to the world how sick she was, so on opening night an assistant bundled her into a chair on wheels and rolled her across the street to the party before anyone else arrived. Even Lola did not know how ill her daughter was.

By the end of November, Wasserstein was in Sloane-Kettering Memorial Cancer Center, receiving chemotherapy for the lymphoma that had spread to her brain. She was in and out of consciousness for six weeks, and on January 30, 2006, she died.

At a memorial service on March 13, 2006, Wasserstein's family of theater colleagues and theatergoers packed the Vivian Beaumont Theater at Lincoln Center. Christopher Durang spoke about his friend with humor, which he knew she would have insisted upon, and tenderness:

"In *The Heidi Chronicles*, Peter says 'I want to know you all my life.' During Wendy's last months, that phrase kept coming back to me. It's very hard to let go of Wendy . . . she had an inner light that came not from her being smart, but from her being an extraordinarily loving and warm woman, and spirit. With Wendy gone, we are all bereft."

After Wasserstein, Who?

The late *New York Times* theater critic Mel Gussow, in one of the last essays he undertook, wrote about three playwrights—Wendy Wasserstein, Marsha Norman, and Beth Henley—who had not only written excellent plays but had also seen them travel to Broadway. "Henley, Norman, and Wasserstein demonstrated—nd it always needs demonstrating—that art can have a life in the marketplace," he noted. Indeed, in evaluating Wasserstein's legacy, one of the most important points to remember is that she proved that a woman's plays could thrive on Broadway, something that had not happened in the American theater since Lillian Hellman wrote from the late 1930s to the 1950s.

But Gussow, who had reviewed or seen all of Wasserstein's major plays except *Third*, also wrote that "Subsequent plays by Henley, Norman, and Wasserstein have not yet equaled their initial success. The playwrights seem fated to be known primarily for the plays that brought them their first fame."

Her plays are very much of her time and her world, which was upper-middle-class, urban, Jewish, and white. Only one of her key plays, *An American Daughter*, has a person of color among the characters. Given that circumscribed universe, it would not be surprising if her best plays no longer spoke to contemporary audiences. But they do. *Uncommon Women* still strikes chords with college-age women trying to forge lives and careers. *The Heidi Chronicles* can still affect women who believe they should "have it all" and mourn that they don't. *The Sisters Rosensweig* remains a funny, touching exploration of female friendship and communication. As for *An American Daughter* and *Third*, one suspects that, given fresh directorial eyes and new productions, they, too, might have authentic messages for contemporary American society.

She was never a radical feminist, nor did she want to be—a truth that apparently irritated many feminists who were. Interestingly, some feminist critics who once decried her plays have reevaluated Wasserstein's work and influence. The outstanding theorist Jill Dolan, in an essay posted on-line after Wasserstein died, wrote what amounts to a feminist eulogy:

"Wasserstein's humor contributed to feminist discourse in the theatre in numerous ways. Her plays are simply funny, and tweak the stereotype of feminists as humorless and strident. She wrote bright, comic plays with a twinge of sadness, melancholy that became more evident and more cutting as her career went on . . . .

"Who will fill her shoes, as a popular, commercially successful woman playwright unafraid to at least address feminism by name, as well as by concept and conceit, courageous enough to look at women's lives and insist that they be the universal to which other human beings can relate and aspire, empathize and identify? . . . . [W]ho will gain the power to tell some of our stories on Broadway, as she's done so consistently all these years? Who will replace her as a public humorist, as someone to be counted on to laugh at our foibles as human beings from the perspective of women in a way that Broadway audiences can find accessible, as well as maybe provoking and just a little bit challenging?

"If Wendy Wasserstein's goal was to assimilate, she did it very well, and carved a path for women in the theatre that we have to be careful doesn't close up after her. She'll be missed."

DRAMATIC MOMENTS FROM THE MAJOR PLAYS

Uncommon Women and Others (1977)

The Heidi Chronicles (1987)

Third (2005)

from *Uncommon Women and Others* (1977)
from Act Two, Scene 2

[*Uncommon Women and Others* is a memory play about women undergraduates at an elite women's college. In this scene from Act Two, Muffet, whom the playwright describes as "an attractive woman, wry and cheerful," and Leilah, "tailored almost to the point of rigidity," talk lightly but anxiously about what they will do after they graduate. Mrs. Plumm, mentioned in the scene, is the overzealous woman in charge of their dorm.]

CHARACTERS
Man (Voiceover)
Muffet
Leilah
Girl (Voiceover)

MAN'S VOICE: In the growth of tradition from the time of its founding by Mary Lyon to the present day, the college continues to believe that the acquisition of knowledge of itself is not enough. Indeed, employers of graduates of the college seem to be looking for a readiness to work hard at learning unfamiliar techniques.

(MUFFET *is putting on makeup.* LEILAH *enters carrying a chocolate bunny.*)

LEILAH: Muffy, this package just came for you.

MUFFET: What is this? (*She reads the gift note.*) "For my Muffet. I can't bluff it. An Easter bunny for my pixie honey."

These short excerpts are from the playwright's major plays. They give a taste of the work of the playwright. Each has a short introduction in brackets that helps the reader understand the context of the excerpt. The excerpts, which are in chronological order by world premiere date, illustrate the main themes mentioned in the In an Hour essay.

LEILAH: Is that from Susie Friend?

MUFFET: Christ, no! It's from her father. Look, it's signed—Lovens, E. Courtland "Kippy" Friend. He was behind me in the bunny hop at Father-Daughter weekend. Leilah, do you think I should plan to marry Kippy Friend? It's two months before graduation and I still don't know what I'm going to do next year. But I am prepared for life. I can fold my napkin with the best of them. Leilah, do you want this? I'll give it to Holly; she'll eat it.

LEILAH: I asked my father not to come up this year. Actually, my freshman year he came to Father-Daughter weekend and kept dancing with Katie and telling me how lucky I was to have such a good friend. Kate told him I was the prettiest and the brightest girl here. Ever since then, I've made it a point to be busy doing research every Father-Daughter weekend. (*Throws down her books.*) Oh, I can't wait to get out of here. I've booked a flight to Iraq for the day after graduation.

MUFFET: Really, Leilah, that's odd. You're very odd.

LEILAH: I won a fellowship.

MUFFET: Pink Pants is leaving right after graduation also. Lei, if he calls, would you tell him I went away for the weekend? We had another fight yesterday.

LEILAH: What happened?

MUFFET: Nothing. He told me that next year he wants to work his way around the world on a freighter. I tried to appear like "sure," "that's fine," "have a nice trip," "send a postcard." I don't understand why Samantha meets someone, suddenly she's pinned, and when I want someone, they tell me I'm being clutchy and putting too much pressure on them. I don't want any commitment, I like being alone.

LEILAH: Me too.

MUFFET: Leilah, where do women meet men after college? Does Paul Weiss Rifkind have mixers with Time/Life staffers at the

General Foods media department?

LEILAH: I don't' know who I'll meet in Iraq. I like that. Katie says I'm escaping. I think I just need to be in a less competitive culture.

MUFFET: Why does Katie bother you so much?

LEILAH: Excuse me?

MUFFET: I can't understand why Katie bothers you so much.

LEILAH: She doesn't. I like Katie. She's exceptional.

MUFFET: Katie has no hips.

LEILAH: It could be Social Darwinism. Katie could simply be a superior creature.

MUFFET: Pink Pants says you're prettier than Katie.

LEILAH: Sometimes when I'm in the library studying, I look up and I count the Katies and the Leilahs. They're always together. And they seem a very similar species. But if you observe a while longer, the Katies seem kind of magical, and the Leilahs are highly competent. And they're usually such good friends—really the best. But I find myself secretly hoping that when we leave here, Katie and I will just naturally stop speaking. There's just something…(*Begins to cry.*) It's not Katie's fault! Sometimes I wonder if it's normal for one twenty-year-old woman to be so constantly aware of another woman…."Thoughts of a dry brain in a dry season."

MUFFET: Mrs. Plumm thinks about Ada Grudder often.

LEILAH: But if we did stop speaking, she wouldn't even notice, or if she did, she'd just think she wasn't a good person for a day. I just want to get out of here so I'm not with people who know me in terms of her.

MUFFET: Leilah, why don't' you come out with me tonight? I've always wanted to do this. We can go to a bar—not too sleazy, but also not a place where two nice girls usually go. And we'll sit alone, just you and I, with our two Brandy Alexanders, and we won't need any outside attention. We'll be two *Uncommon Women*, mysterious but proud. (*Puts her arm around* LEILAH.)

LEILAH: All right. I'd like that.

MUFFET: Leilah, I do understand a little. It's debilitating constantly seeing your worth in terms of someone else.

GIRL'S VOICE: Male LD for Muffet Di Nicola. Muffet Di Nicola, Male LD.

LEILAH: I'll take it for you, Muffy.

MUFFET (*Pauses and then gets her coat.*) No. It's got to be Old Pink Pants. Would you sign an overnight slip for me? See, Leilah, I know myself, and as soon as the phone rings, I'm just fine. (*Exits with her coat.*)

(LEILAH *is left alone in the room holding the chocolate bunny.*)

from *The Heidi Chronicles* (1987)
from Act One, Scene 2

[In this scene from Wendy Wasserstein's Pulitzer Prize-winning play, young, idealistic Heidi Holland meets the young, cynical journalist Scoop Rosenbaum at a campaign event for the would-be Democratic Presidential candidate Senator Eugene McCarthy. The repartee is Wasserstein at her best, in a scene that suggests both Heidi's inner conflicts and the pair's mutual sexual attraction.]

CHARACTERS
Scoop Rosenbaum
Heidi Holland

(*1968. A dance. There are "Eugene McCarthy for President" signs. "Take a Piece of My Heart" by Janis Joplin and Big Brother and the Holding Company, can be heard. A hippie in a Sergeant Pepper jacket smokes a joint. When* HEIDI *enters, he offers her a drag.* HEIDI, *wearing a floral shawl, refuses and stands by the food table.* SCOOP ROSENBAUM, *intense but charismatic, in blue jeans and work shirt, goes over to her. He takes a beer from a bucket on stage.*)

SCOOP: Are you guarding the chips?

HEIDI: No.

SCOOP: Then you're being very difficult.

HEIDI: Please, help yourself.

SCOOP: Where are you going?

HEIDI: I'm trying to listen to the music.

SCOOP: Janis Joplin and Big Brother and the Holding Company. A-singer. C + band. Far less innovative than the Kinks. You know, you really have one hell of an inferiority complex.

HEIDI: I do?

SCOOP: Sure. I have no right to say you're difficult. Don't you believe in human dignity? I mean, you're obviously a liberal, or you wouldn't be here.

HEIDI: I came with a friend.

SCOOP: You came to Manchester, New Hampshire, in a blizzard to ring doorbells for Gene McCarthy because of a friend? Why the fuck didn't you go skiing instead?

HEIDI: I don't ski.

SCOOP: (*Offers* HEIDI *a potato chip.*) B- texture, C + crunch. You go to one of those Seven Sister schools?

HEIDI: How did you know?

SCOOP: You're all concerned citizens.

HEIDI: I told you, I came because of a friend.

SCOOP: That's bullshit. Be real. You're neat and clean for Eugene. You think if you go door to door and ring bells, this sucker will become president, and we'll all be good people, and wars in places you've never heard of before will end, and everyone will have enough to eat and send their daughters to Vassar. Like I said, neat and clean for Eugene.

HEIDI: Would you excuse me?

SCOOP: (*Smiles and extends his hand to her.*) It's been lovely chatting with me.

HEIDI: A pleasure.

SCOOP: What's your name?

HEIDI: Susan.

SCOOP: Susan what?

HEIDI: Susan Johnston. See ya.

SCOOP: Hey, Susan Johnston, wouldn't you like to know who I am?

HEIDI: Uh…

SCOOP: C'mon. Nice girl like you isn't going to look a man in the eye and tell him, "I have absolutely no interest in you. You've been incredibly obnoxious and your looks are B-."

HEIDI: Why do you grade everything?

SCOOP: I used to be a very good student.

HEIDI: Used to?

SCOOP: I dropped out of Princeton. The Woodrow Wilson School of International Bullshit.

HEIDI: So what do you do now?

SCOOP: This and That. Here and there.

HEIDI: You work for McCarthy? Well, you *are* at a McCarthy dance.

SCOOP: I came with a friend. Susan, don't you know this is just the tip of the iceberg? McCarthy is irrelevant. He's a C + Adlai Stevenson. The changes in this country could be enormous. Beyond anything your sister mind can imagine.

HEIDI: Are you a real-life radical?

SCOOP: You mean, do I make bombs in my parents' West Hartford basement? Susan, how could I be a radical? I played lacrosse at Exeter and I'm a Jew whose first name is Scoop. You're not very good at nuance. And you're too eager to categorize. I'm a journalist. I'm just here to have a look around.

HEIDI: Do you work for a paper?

SCOOP: Did they teach you at Vassar to ask so many inane questions in order to keep a conversation going?

HEIDI: Well, like I said, I have to meet my friend.

SCOOP: Me too. I have to meet Paul Newman.

HEIDI: Please tell him Susan says "Hi."

SCOOP: You don't believe I have to meet Paul Newman.

HEIDI: I'm sure you do.

SCOOP: I'm picking him up at the airport and taking him and Mr.

McCarthy to a press conference. Paul's a great guy. Why don't you come drinking with us? We can rap over a few brews.

HEIDI: I'm sorry. I can't.

SCOOP: Why not?

HEIDI: I just can't.

SCOOP: Susan, let me get this straight. You would rather drive back to Poughkeepsie with five virgins in a Volkswagen discussing Norman Mailer and birth control dangerous frozen roads than go drinking with Eugene McCarthy, Paul Newman, and Scoop Rosenbaum? You're cute, Susan. Very cute.

HEIDI: And you are really irritating!

SCOOP: That's the first honest thing you've said all night! Lady, you better learn to stand up for yourself. I'll let you in on a scoop from Scoop.

HEIDI: Did they teach you construction like that at Princeton?

SCOOP: I dig you, Susan. I dig you a lot.

HEIDI: Can we say "like" instead of "dig"? I mean, while I am standing up for myself…

SCOOP: I like you, Susan. You're prissy, but I like you a lot.

HEIDI: Well, I don't know if I like you.

SCOOP: Why should you like me? I'm arrogant and difficult. But I'm very smart. So you'll put up with me. What?

HEIDI: What what?

SCOOP: You're thinking something.

HEIDI: Actually, I was wondering what mothers teach their sons that they never bother to tell their daughters.

SCOOP: What do you mean?

HEIDI: I mean, why the fuck are you so confident?

SCOOP: Ten points for Susan!

HEIDI: Have we moved on to points, from letter grades?

SCOOP: There's hope for you. You're going to be quite the little politico.

HEIDI: I'm planning to be an art historian.

SCOOP: Please don't say that. That's really suburban.

HEIDI: I'm interested in the individual expression of the human soul. Content over form.

SCOOP: But I thought the point of contemporary art is that form becomes the content. Look at Albers' Homage to a Square." Three superimposed squares, and we're talking perception, integration, isolation. Just three squares, and they reflect the gross inadequacies of our society. Therefore, your argument is inconclusive.

HEIDI: Don't give me a Marxist interpretation of Albers.

SCCOP: You really are one fuck of a liberal! Next thing you'll tell me is how much Herbert Marcuse means to you. What?

HEIDI: Nothing.

SCOOP: I don't fuckin' believe it! You've never read Marcuse!

HEIDI: Isn't Paul Newman waiting for you, Scoop?

SCOOP: Isn't your friend waiting for you, *Heidi? (Jumps up.)* Basket, Rosenbaum. Thirty points. The score is 30 to 10.

HEIDI: How did you know my name?

SCOOP: I told you I'm a journalist. Do you really think anything *(Takes out the paper to show her.)* gets by the *Liberated Earth News*?

HEIDI: That's your paper?

SCOOP: Editor in chief. Circulation 362 and growing. Okay. Truth. I know your name is Heidi because it says so right here *(Looks in the paper and then up at her breast.)* on your name tag. Heidi. H-E-I-D-I.

HEIDI: Oh!

SCOOP: Ohh!

HEIDI: Oh, well…(*Begins to pull the tag off.*)

SCOOP: You don't have to look at the floor.

HEIDI: I'm not.

SCOOP: I've got nothing on you so far. Why are you so afraid to speak up?

HEIDI: I'm not afraid to speak up.

SCOOP: Heidi, you don't understand. You're the one this is all going to affect. You're the one whose life this will all change significantly. Has to. You're a very serious person. In fact, you're the unfortunate contradiction in terms—a serious good person. And I envy you that.

HEIDI: Thank you. I guess.

SCOOP: Yup. You'll be one of those true believers who didn't understand it was all just a phase. The Trotskyite during Lenin's New Economic Policy. The worshipper of fallen images in Christian Judea.

HEIDI: And you?

SCOOP: Me? I told you. I'm just here to have a look around.

HEIDI: What if you get left behind?

SCOOP: You mean if, after all the politics, you girls decide to go "hog wild," demanding equal pay, equal rights, equal orgasms?

HEIDI: All people deserve to fulfill their potential.

SCOOP: Absolutely.

HEIDI: I mean, why should some well-educated woman waste her life making you and your children tuna-fish sandwiches?

SCOOP: She shouldn't. And, for that matter, neither should a badly educated woman. Heidella, I'm on your side.

HEIDI: Don't' call me Heidella. It's diminutive.

SCOOP: You mean "demeaning," and it's not. It's endearing.

HEIDI: You're deliberately eluding my train of thought.

SCOOP: No. I'm subtly asking you to go to bed with me…before I go meet Paul Newman.

(*Pause.*)

HEIDI: Oh.

SCOOP: You have every right to say no. I can't guarantee absolute equality of experience.

HEIDI: I can take care of myself, thanks.

SCOOP: You're already got the lingo down, kiddo. Pretty soon you'll be burning bras.

HEIDI: Maybe I'll go "hog wild."

SCOOP: I hope so. Are you a virgin?

HEIDI: Excuse me?

SCOOP: If you choose to accept this invitation, I'll find out one way or the other.

HEIDI: (*Embarrassed.*) That's okay.

SCOOP: Why do you cover your mouth when you talk about sex?

HEIDI: Hygiene.

SCOOP: (*Takes her hand away from her mouth.*) I told you. You're a serious good person. And I'm honored. Maybe you'll think fondly of all this in some Proustian haze when you're thirty-five and picking your daughter up from Ethical Culture School to escort her to cello class before dinner with Dad, the noted psychiatrist and Miró poster collector.

HEIDI: No. I'll be busy torching lingerie.

SCOOP: Maybe I'll remember it one day when I'm thirty-five and watching my son's performance as Johnny Appleseed. Maybe I'll look at my wife, who puts up with me, and flash on when I was editor of a crackpot liberal newspaper and thought I could fall in love with Heidi Holland, the canvassing art historian, that first snowy night in Manchester, New Hampshire, 1968.

HEIDI: Are you guarding the chips?

SCOOP: No. I trust them.

(*He kisses her passionately as "White Rabbit" begins playing.* SCOOP *then looks at his watch and gathers his coat. He begins to leave the room and turns back to* HEIDI. *She looks at her watch and follows him. He clenches his fist in success.*)

from *The Heidi Chronicles* (1987)
from Act Two, Scene 4

[In this famous monologue from *The Heidi Chronicles,* Heidi Holland, now in her late thirties, describes her deep disappointment with the Women's Movement in which she and many other women had placed so much faith. Despite her independence and her accomplishments, Heidi feels "stranded."]

CHARACTERS
Sandra Zucker-Hall (Voiceover)
Heidi Holland

(*1986. The Plaza Hotel. We hear the voice-over of* SANDRA ZUCKER-HALL.)

SANDRA: Good Afternoon. I'm Sandra Zucker-Hall, president of the Miss Crain's School East Coast Alumnae Association. The topic for today's luncheon is "Women, Where Are We Going," and we are very pleased to have as our speaker a distinguished alumna, Dr. Heidi Holland.

HEIDI: (*Very well dressed, stands behind a lectern.*) Hello. Hello. I graduated from Miss Crain's in 1965, and I look back on my education in Chicago very fondly. One of the far-reaching habits I developed at Miss Crain's was waiting until the desperation point to complete or, rather, start, my homework. Keeping that noble academic tradition alive, I appear before you today with no formal speech. I have no outline, no pink note cards, no hieroglyphics scribbled on my palm. Nothing. Well, you might be thinking, this is a women's meeting, so let's give her the benefit of the doubt. After teaching at Columbia yesterday, Miss Holland probably attended a low-impact aerobics class *with* weights, picked up her children from school, took the older one to drawing-with-computers at the Metropolitan, and the younger one to swimming-for-gifted-children. On returning home, she immediately prepared grilled mesquite free-range chicken with balsamic vinegar and sun-dried tomatoes, advised her investment-banker well-rounded husband on future finances for the City Ballet, put the children to bed, recited their favorite Greek myths and sex-education legends, dashed into the library to call the twenty-two-year-old squash player who is passionately in love with her to say that they can only be friends, finished writing ten pages of a new book, took the remains of the mesquite free-range dinner to a church that feeds the homeless, massaged her husband's feet, and relieved any fears that he "might" be getting old by "doing it" in the kitchen, read forty pages of the *Inferno* in Italian, took a deep breath, and put out the light. So after all this, we forgive Miss Holland for not preparing a speech today. She's exemplary and exhausted. Thank you, but you forgive too easily. And I respect my fellow alumnae enough to know that I should attempt to tell you the truth. Oh, hurry up, Heidi. Okay. Why don't I have a speech for the "Women, Where Are We Going" luncheon? Well, actually, yesterday I did teach at Columbia. We discussed Alexander Pope and his theory of the picturesque. And afterward I did attend an exercise class. I walked into the locker room, to my favorite corner, where I can pull on my basic black leotard in peace. Two ladies, younger than me, in pressed blue jeans, were heatedly debating the reading program at Marymount nursery school, and a woman my mother's age was going on and on about her son at Harvard Law School and his wife, a Brazilian hairdresser, who was by no stretch of the imagination good enough for him. They were joined by Mrs. Green, who has perfect red nails, and confessed to anyone who would listen the hardship of throwing her dinner party on the same night as a benefit at the Met. And in the middle of them was a naked gray-haired woman extolling the virtues of brown rice and women's fiction. And then two twenty-seven-year-old hot-shots came in. How do I know they were hotshots? They were both draped in purple and green leather. And as soon as they entered the locker room, they pulled out their alligator date-books and began madly to call the office. They seemed to have everything under control. They even brought their own heavier weights. Now Jeanette, the performance-artist-dancer-actress-aerobics teacher, comes in and completes the locker room. I like Jeanette. I've never talked to her, but I like her. I feel her parents are psychiatrists in the Midwest. Maybe Cedar Rapids. Jeanette takes off her blue jeans and rolls her tights up her legs. I notice the hotshots checking out Jeanette's muscle tone while they are lacing up their Zeus low-impact sneakers, and Mrs. Green stops talking about her dinner party to ask where did they find them. Everywhere she has looked on Madison Avenue is out. And the lady with the son at Harvard joins in and says she saw Zeus sneakers at Lord and Taylor and were they any good. Her daughter-in-law likes them, but she can't be trusted. The mothers with the pressed blue jeans leap to her rescue. Yes, they can assure her, despite the daughter-in-law, unequivocally, absolutely, no doubt about it, Zeus sneakers are the best! It was at this point that I decided I would slip out take my place in the back row of the class. I packed up my overstuffed bag. But as I was just between Mrs. Green's raccoon coat and a purple leather bomber jacket, I tripped on one of the shotshots' goddamn five-pound professional weights, and out of my bag flew a week's worth of change, raspberry gum wrappers, and *Alexander Pope on the Picturesque* right on the naked gray-haired fiction woman's foot. I began giggling. "Oh." "That's okay." "Excuse me." "I'm sorry." "I'm sorry I don't wear leather pants." "I'm sorry I don't eat brown rice." "I'm sorry I don't want to stand naked and discuss Zeus sneakers." "I'm sorry I don't want you to find out I'm worthless. And superior." I'm embarrassed—no, humiliated—in front of every woman in that room. I'm envying women I don't even know. I'm envying women I don't even like. I'm sure the woman with the son at Harvard is miserable to her daughter-in-law. I'm sure the gray-haired fiction woman is having a bisexual relationship with a female dockworker and driving her husband crazy. I'm sure the hotshots have screwed a lot of thirty-five-year-old women, my classmates even, out of jobs, raises, and husbands. And I'm sure the mothers in the pressed blue jeans think women like me chose the wrong road. "Oh, it's a pity they made such a mistake, that empty generation." Well, I really don't want to be feeling this way about all of them. And I certainly don't want to be feeling this way about "Women, Where Are We Going." I hear whispers. I hear chairs moving from side to side. Yes, I see. I have one minute left. The women start filing out of the locker room Jeannette ties her hair in a ponytail and winks at me. "See you in class, Heidi. Don't forget to take a mat this time." And I look at her pink and kind face. "I'm sorry," Jeannette, I think I'm too sad to go to class." "Excuse me?" She smiles and grabs a mat. And suddenly I stop competing with all of them. Suddenly I'm not even racing. "To tell you the truth, Jeanette, I think I better not exercise today." "Is there anything I can do?" She puts her arm around me. "Are you not well?" "No, Jeanette. I'm just not happy. I'm afraid I haven't been happy for some time."

(*Looks up at the audience.*)

I don't blame the ladies in the locker room for how I feel. I don't blame any of us. We're all concerned, intelligent, good women. (*Pauses.*) It's just that I feel stranded. And I thought the whole point was that we wouldn't feel stranded. I thought the point was that we were all in this together. Thank you.

(*Walks off.*)

from *Third* (2005)
from Act Two, Scene 5

[Laurie, the central character of Wasserstein's last major play, *Third,* is an English literature professor at an Ivy League college. She has had a difficult semester, but here, in this delicate scene toward the play's end, we see Laurie's compassionate side as she helps her elderly, senile father, who has wandered away from home. Wasserstein's own father, who had died a few years before this play was written, had suffered from dementia.]

CHARACTERS
Jack
Laurie

(*Early May. Outside the college bookstore. It's a stormy night. Jack enters.*)

JACK: Hello? Hello? Who's there? We're coming ashore! Tell those goddamn bastards that Jack Jameson is here! Tell them that I'm not afraid of Saddam or anyone. I'm an American, goddamn it. You can't fool me. I'm Jack Jameson. (*Laurie enters.*)

LAURIE: Dad? Dad?

JACK: Who are you?

LAURIE: It's Laurie, Daddy.

JACK: Laurie? Do you live near here?

LAURIE: Close by.

JACK: That's nice. Thank you for coming. Would you like to sit down?

LAURIE: Dad, let me take you home.

JACK: I don't want to go home. I like being on the bow of this ship.

I can see land over there. Why don't you sit with me? You have a very nice face.

LAURIE: Thank you.

JACK: I came to America in a boat like this. I was six years old and lived in Amsterdam. My father had left a few years earlier to work in his cousin's toy store in Delaware. I came here with my cousin and my sister. I got married here, I took over the business, and I had three children: two girls and a boy. Am I boring you?

LAURIE: No.

JACK: Do you have any children?

LAURIE: Two girls. Zooey and Emily.

JACK: My daughters' names are Maryann and Laurie. Maryann lives in Denver, and Laurie looks just like Marilyn Monroe.

LAURIE: Oh, Dad.

JACK: But she's very smart, my daughter Laurie. Talks all the time. Blah blah blah. You know what I mean?

LAURIE: I think so.

JACK: Listen, don't get me wrong, there are a lot of bastards out there. But nobody's always right. Am I right? I can't hear you.

LAURIE: Dad, it's cold out here.

JACK: So, zip up your jacket. Stay a while. What's your hurry?

LAURIE: Honey, it's midnight. We've been looking for you all night.

JACK: I can count backwards from a hundred. Want to hear?

LAURIE: Daddy.

JACK: A hundred, ninety-nine, ninety-eight…Goddamn it. What happens after ninety-eight? Goddamn it. I just had it. The goddamn bastards took it away from me.

LAURIE: It' ninety-seven.

JACK: Really? That's nice. Ninety-seven. You're very generous.

LAURIE: It's fine, really.

JACK: No, I really want to thank you. And I hope I haven't been too much of a burden.

LAURIE: You're not a burden.

JACK: Yes I am. Listen to me. Sometimes, you just need to say I'm sorry.

LAURIE: What?

JACK: I want to set the record straight. I just want to say that I'm sorry.

LAURIE: You don't have to.

JACK: But I want to. And you owe me the courtesy to accept my apology. I'm a good boy but I couldn't control my behavior, but I am sorry about it.

LAURIE: Dad—

JACK: Just accept my apology. (*She takes his hand.*)

LAURIE: All right Dad, I accept your apology.

JACK: I love you very much. What we have is very good. Do you agree?

LAURIE: Yes, very good. It's cold. I should take you home.

JACK: Do you live very far from here?

LAURIE: No, near here.

JACK: That's nice. I don't live here. My daughter does. Would you like to meet her? I think you and she would get along.

LAURIE: Yes.

JACK: I have to go to work tomorrow. I have a toy store in Wilmington. This is our busy season. But after Christmas, maybe you and my daughter could get together with me. I think you would like her. She's got stuff.

LAURIE: Sure, call me. C'mon. (*She helps him up.*)

JACK: Do you like to dance?

LAURIE: What?

JACK: It stopped raining. And the stars are out. I like to dance.

LAURIE: But…

JACK: I know I just met you, but I don't know how many more dances I have left. Do you like Benny Goodman?

LAURIE: My father really liked Benny Goodman.

JACK: Then let's think of your father and dance to him. (*He speaks-sings the first few bars of "Moonglow."*) "It must have been Moonglow, Way up in the blue. It must have been Moonglow, That led me straight to you."

(*They dance.*)

WASSERSTEIN: THE READING ROOM

Young Actors and Their Teachers

Backes, Nancy. "Wasserstein, Wendy." In *Notable Women in the American Theatre,* edited by Alice M. Robinson, Vera Mowry Roberts, and Milly S. Barranger. Westport, CT: Greenwood Press, Inc. 1989.

Kolin, Phillp C. "Wendy Wasserstein." In *American Playwrights Since 1945: A Guide to Scholarship, Criticism, and Performance.* Westport, Connecticut: Greenwood Press, 1989.

Scholars, Students, Professors

Balakian, Jan. "Wendy Wasserstein: A Feminist Voice from the Seventies to the Present." In *The Cambridge Companion to American Women Playwrights,* edited by Brenda Murphy, pp. 213-31. Cambridge: Cambridge University Press, 1999.

_____. *Reading the Plays of Wendy Wasserstein.* New York: Applause Theatre and Cinema Books, 2010.

Barnett, Claudia, ed. *Wendy Wasserstein: A Casebook.* New York: Garland, 1999.

Betsko, Kathleen, and Rachel Koenig. *Interviews with Contemporary Women Playwrights.* New York: William Morrow and Company, Inc., 1987.

This extensive bibliography lists books about the playwright according to whom the books might be of interest. The books are grouped as follows: Young Actors and Their Teachers; Scholars, Students, Professors; Theaters, Producers; and Actors, Directors, Theater Professionals. If you want to track down something that interested you in the text, you can find the references in this section

Bryer, Jackson R., ed. "Wendy Wasserstein." In *The Playwright's Art: Conversations with Contemporary American Dramatists*. New Brunswick, N.J.: Rutgers University Press, 1995.

Carlson, Susan L. "Comic Textures and Female Communities 1937 and 1977: Clare Boothe and Wendy Wasserstein." In *Modern Drama,* Vol. 27, December 1984, pp. 564–73.

Cattaneo, Anne. "When Comedy Is Commercial: Wasserstein and Durang." *Theatre Crafts* (November-December 1984):32, 85-87.

Chinoy, Helen Krich, and Linda Walsh Jenkins. *Women in the American Theatre.* New York: Theatre Communications Group, 2006.

Canning, Charlotte. *Feminist Theaters in the U.S.A.* London: Routledge, 1996.

Chirico, Miriam M. "Female Laughter and Comic Possibilities: *Uncommon Women and Others*." In *Modern Dramatists: A Casebook of Major British, Irish, and American Playwrights,* edited by Kimball King, pp. 339-59. New York: Routledge, 2001.

Cohen, Esther. "Uncommon Woman: An Interview with Wendy Wasserstein." *Women's Studies* 15, nos. 1-3 (1988): 257-70.

Crane, Gladys. "Playwriting Images to Improve Women's Position." *Indiana Theatre Bulletin* (February 1983): 11-13.

Donahue, Richard. "Opening Night." *Publishers Weekly* 243, no. 17 (22 April 1996).

Jenkins, Jeffrey Eric, ed. *The Best Plays* series. Pompton Plains, NJ: Limelight Editions.

Kennedy, Pagan. *Platforms: A Microwaved Cultural Chronicle of the 1970s.* (New York: St. Martin's Press, 1994.

Keyssar, Helene. "Drama and the Dialogic Imagination: *The Heidi Chronicles* and *Fefu and Her Friends.*" *Modern Drama* 34, no. 1 (March 1991): 88-106.

Luce, Clare Boothe. *The Women.* New York: Dramatists Play Service, Inc., 1998.

Ortner, Sherry. *Making Gender: The Politics and Erotics of Cutlure.* Boston: Beacon Books, 1996.

Swain, Elizabeth. "Wendy Wasserstein." In *Contemporary Dramatists.* 4th ed., pp. 547-49. Edited by D.L. Kirkpatrick. Chicago: St. James Press, 1988.

Whitfield, Stephen J. "Wendy Wasserstein and the Crisis of (Jewish) Identity." In *Daughters of Valor: Contemporary Jewish American Women Writers,* edited by Jay L. Halio and Ben Siegel, pp. 226-46. Newark: University of Delaware Press, 1997.

Wolfe, Tom. *The Bonfire of the Vanities.* New York: Bantam, 1988.

Theaters, Producers

Goldman, William. *The Season.* New York: Harcourt, Brace & World, Inc., 1969.

Kantor, Michael, and Laurence Maslon. *Broadway: The American Musical.* Boston: Bulfinch, 2004.

Rich, Frank. *Hot Seat: Theater Criticism for "The New York Times," 1980-1993.* New York: Random House, 1998.

Actors, Directors, Theater Professionals

Alper, J. et al. "Dramaturgies in America; 11 Statements and Discussion." *Theater 10* (1978-1979): 15-30.

Hagen, Uta. *Respect for Acting.* New York: Macmillan,1973.

Editions of Wasserstein's Plays Used for this Book

Wasserstein, Wendy. *The Heidi Chronicles, Uncommon Women and Others* & *Isn't It Romantic.* New York: Vintage Books, 1991.

_____. *The Sisters Rosensweig.* New York: Harcourt Brace and Company, 1993.

_____. *Seven One-Act Plays.* New York: Dramatists Play Service Inc., 2000.

_____. *An American Daughter*. New York: Dramatists Play Service Inc., 2001.

_____. *Old Money.* New York: Harcourt Brace and Company, 2002.

_____. *Third.* New York: Dramatists Play Service Inc., 2008.

Sources Cited in this Book

Austin, Gayle. "A Review of *The Heidi Chronicles.*" *Theatre Journal* (March 1990): 107-08.

Brantley, Ben. "In the Hostile Glare of Washington, the Media Define and Defy." *New York Times* (14 April 1997).

Dolan, Jill. "Wendy Wasserstein, In Memoriam." *The Feminist Spectator.* http://feministspectator.blogspot.com/2006/01/wendy-wasserstein-in-memoriam.html

Durang, Christopher. Interviews with Alexis Greene. August, September, and October 2011.

Eder, Richard. "Dramatic Wit and Wisdom Unite in '*Uncommon Women and Others.*'" New York Times (22 November 1977).

Greene, Alexis. "Joking Aside: A Conversation about Comedy with Christopher Durang, Gina Gionfriddo, Sarah Ruhl, and Wendy Wasserstein." In *Women Writing Plays: Three Decades of the Susan Smith Blackburn Prize,* edited by Alexis Greene. Austin, Texas: University of Texas Press, 2006.

Gussow, Mel. "Women Playwrights: New Voices in the Theater." *New York Times Magazine* (1 May 1983).

_____. "Stage: New 'Romantic' by Wendy Wasserstein." New York Times (16 December 1983).

_____. "A Modern-Day Heffalump in Search of Herself." *New York Times* (12 December 1988).

_____. "Wasserstein: Comedy, Character, Reflection." *New York Times* (23 October 1992).

_____. "Entering the Mainstream: The Plays of Beth Henley, Marsha Norman, and Wendy Wasserstein." In *Women Writing Plays: Three Decades of the Susan Smith Blackburn Prize,* edited by Alexis Greene. Austin, Texas: University of Texas Press, 2006.

Henry, William. Review of "*The Heidi Chronicles. Time* Magazine (19 March 1989).

Kalem, T. E. "Stereotopical." Times (5 December 1977).

Keyssar, Helene. *Feminist Theatre*. New York: Grove Press, 1985.

Oliver, Edith. *The New Yorker* (5 December 1977).

_____. *The New Yorker.* (26 December 1983).

Ouderkirk, Cathleen Stinson. "Human Connections—A Playwright's View: Wendy Wasserstein discusses '*The Heidi Chronicles.*'" *The Christian Science Monitor* (10 October 1989).

Salamon, Julie. *Wendy and the Lost Boys*. New York: The Penguin Press, 2011.

Simon, John. "The Group." *New York* Magazine (12 December 1977).

_____. "*The Heidi Chronicles*." *New York* Magazine (19 March 1989).